# Name Change
# *(Adult or Minor)*

*do it yourself*

# A Step By Step Guide

## LawPak's Commitment and Goal

The goal of LawPak is to simplify legal information for consumers. Our LawPak's contain accurate, easy-to-read information and forms.

LawPak is committed to designing the highest quality forms and guides. We believe that non-lawyers should have access to legal information that has been researched and professionally prepared. Our books can save the non-lawyer unnecessary legal expenses in providing information to better understand their legal problem.

We will guarantee replacement of any LawPak in which you find defective materials. However, we cannot guarantee that the way you complete the forms will be correct for your circumstances. Please be aware that laws and procedures are constantly changing and are subject to differing interpretations.

We can guarantee that we have used extensive efforts to provide you with clear instructions and forms as that you may have the opportunity to learn about legal procedures and handle your own legal matters if you choose to do so. In order to constantly improve our legal forms and LawPaks, we welcome your suggestions and comments.

The LawPak Publishing Professionals

P.O. Box 458
Milford, Ohio 45150

This LawPak book may not be copied, transmitted, transcribed, stored in a retrieval system, or translated into any human or computer language, in any form or by any means, electronic, mechanical, magnetic, chemical, manual, or otherwise, without written permission of the publisher.

**LAWPAK, INC. MAKES NO REPRESENTATION OR WARRANTIES WITH RESPECT TO THE CONTENTS HEREOF AND SPECIFICALLY DISCLAIMS ANY IMPLIED WARRANTIES OF MERCHANTABILITY OR FITNESS FOR ANY PARTICULAR PURPOSE.**

LawPak, Inc. reserves the right to revise this publication and to make changes from time to time in its content without the obligation to notify any person or organization of such revision or changes.

Although care has been taken to ensure the accuracy and utility of the information and forms contained in this book. LawPak, the authors, nor the distributor assume any liability in connection with any use of the information or forms contained herein.

First Edition - 1988

This publication is designed to provide accurate and authoritative information in regard to the subject matter covered. It is sold with the understanding that the publisher is not engaged in rendering legal, accounting, or other professional service. If legal advice or other expert assistance is required, the services of a competent professional person should be sought.

*...From the Declaration of Principles jointly adopted by a committee of the American Bar Association and a Committee of Publishers and Associations.*

Copyright © 1993, LawPak, Inc. All rights reserved.
LawPak is a registered trademark of LawPak Incorporated.
Printed in the United States of America.

**ISBN: 1-879421-00-3**

# Table Of Contents

## Part One

## *All About Name Changes*

**A. Introduction** .................................................... 8
    **A1** - About LawPak
    **A2** - Basic Information
    **A3** - Finding The Right Attorney
    **A4** - Commonly Asked Questions
    **A5** - Advantages of Doing Your Own Name Change
    **A6** - Required Conditions for An Ohio Name Change
    **A7** - Required Waiting Period

**B. Basic Information On Changing Your Name** ................. 14
    **B1** - Methods of Changing Your Name
    **B2** - Names Given at Birth
    **B3** - Names One Cannot Use
    **B4** - Changing Or Not Changing a Woman's Name Upon Marriage
    **B5** - Divorced Women And Name Changes
    **B6** - Children of Divorced Parents And Name Changes

**C. Getting The Name Change Recognized** ..................... 18
    **C1** - Governmental Agencies To Notify
        a. Birth Certificate
        b. Social Security Records
        c. Driver's License/Car Registration
        d. Voting Registration
        e. Income Tax (State, Federal, and Local)
        f. Deeds To Real Estate
        g. Passports
        h. Welfare Payments
        i. Postal Service
        j. Selective Service
        k. Veterans Administration
    **C2** - Important Private Sector Entities to Notify ................ 20
        a. Mortgages
        b. Credit Cards
        c. Bank Accounts
        d. Stocks and Bonds
        e. Wills and Inheritances
        f. Insurance
        g. Telephone Listings
        h. School Records
        i. Professional Associations
        j. Creditors
    **C3** - Other Records to Change ..................................... 21

# Table Of Contents

## Part Two

# *How To Do A Name Change*

1. How to Use The Forms .................................................................... 24
2. Local County Forms ....................................................................... 25
3. How to File The Forms And Set Your Hearing Date ......................... 26
4. The Petition for Name Change of An Adult ..................................... 27
   Setting Petition for Hearing
5. The Notice of Publication ............................................................... 30
   Affidavit
   Entry Ordering Publication
6. The Judgement Entry Ordering The Name Change of An Adult ........ 34
7. The Affidavit In Proof Of Publication ............................................. 36
   Changing A Minor's Name
8. The Petition for Name Change of A Minor ..................................... 38
   Consent To Change Of Name of A Minor
      Mother
      Father
   Setting Petition for Hearing
   Entry Ordering Publication
   Notice By Publication
   Notice to Others
   Entry Ordering The Change Of Name Of A Minor
9. Attending The Hearing .................................................................. 48
10. What Happens If Something Goes Wrong ..................................... 50
11. Check List .................................................................................... 52

**APPENDIX**
Vital Statistics Offices for The Fifty States ........................................ 54

**Blank Forms** .............................................................. 60

    **Adult**

        Petition To Change The Name of An Adult
        Setting Petition For Hearing
        Notice of Publication of Change of Name of An Adult
        Entry Ordering Publication
        Affidavit To Publish
        Judgement Entry Ordering The Name Change of An Adult

    **Minor**

        Petition To Change The Name of A Minor
        Setting Petition For Hearing
        Answer And Consent To Name Change of A Minor
            Mother
            Father
        Notice of Publication of Change of Name of A Minor
        Entry Ordering Publication
        Other Notice
        Judgement Entry Ordering The Name Change of A Minor


Return Card to LawPak For Updates
Other Available LawPaks
Bill of Rights

Abaecherli Adams Ar
Bentley Bieliauskas
Carbonic Corwin Chr
Daley Dalrymple Dav
Economou Edwards
Farris Faybyshev Fie

*Part One*
*All About Name Changes*

# CHAPTER A
## *Introduction*

### A1 About This LawPak

The intent of this LawPak is to assist you in legally changing your name. However, you may use a LawPak as one of many source materials to help you gain a better understanding of your legal needs and still decide to consult with an attorney. LawPaks are written in easy-to-understand language and address the most common questions and procedures concerning changing your name.

Although, LawPak, Inc., is a publishing company and as such does not attempt to form opinions, offer solutions or give legal advice concerning any aspect of your particular situation. The opinions expressed in this book are those of the attorney authors and should not be interpreted as representing those of the entire legal community.

Throughout this LawPak you are advised of situations when you *should* speak with a lawyer. Consult a lawyer if you have *any* doubts about any matter, including anything discussed in the LawPak. It should be noted that certain situations require professional legal assistance.

If you have decided that you can and should do your own Name Change, you should first read this entire book before doing anything. It is written in plain language but read it carefully. Do not do anything unless you fully understand what you want to accomplish.

# A2 Basic And Background Information

Under the legal tradition on which our legal system is based—the common law—which was inherited from England, surnames did not come into wide use until the fourteenth century. At that time these names were chosen at random—and remained valid only during the life of its user. By the time of Queen Elizabeth I, it had become necessary to maintain a record of births, marriages, and deaths through the religious parishes. In the origins of this system a name could be easily changed, and this characteristic has survived to present time.

It remains possible even today for one to change his or her name without aid of a court order. The problem with this particular approach is that various governmental or business agencies with which people deal on a daily basis may require more than a person's word as to what he or she is called. Thus, at some time, a court order or a corrected birth certificate may be necessary to get the name change officially recognized.

# A3 Finding The Right Attorney

LawPaks are not written to replace lawyers. They are intended to give you a basic understanding of your legal situation and offer an affordable option to those individuals who decide that they can do certain legal procedures themselves. You must decide if or when the services of a lawyer may be necessary for your circumstances.

There are not any laws which require you to hire a lawyer to represent you or sign your legal documents. When you represent yourself, you are said to be acting propia persona or the shorter version is pro per which is latin for *yourself*.

If you have some problem with some part of your name change or need additional information, you may decide that a conference with a lawyer would be beneficial. Instead of having a lawyer do the complete name change, you might seek assistance with only part of it.

The best way to find an attorney is through a trusted person who has had a satisfactory experience with one. When you call, don't be intimidated. Ask what their fees would be for a name change (or explain your problem), and how much for an initial interview will cost. Attorney fees vary considerably. Most attorneys will do the first interview for $20 to $30. Hourly rates run from $85 to $300 per hour, with a fee of $300 to $500 being fairly common for a name change.

Before you go to see an attorney, be sure you know exactly what you expect from their services. Have all relevant documents and information with you. As we just mentioned, most attorneys work and charge for their services based upon an hourly rate.

Many federally funded legal aid offices which were created to assist people with low incomes without charge, will **not** normally help you with a name change because a name change case is "fee generating". This means that lawyers (the legal community) object to Legal Aid handling a case for free which could generate a fee to another lawyer working outside of Legal Aid.

# A4 Commonly Asked Questions

**How much will it cost to do my own Name Change?**

A court filing fee (the cost for certified copies of the court order changing your name), the cost of publishing the notice in "a newspaper of general circulation" in the county where you live plus the cost of this LawPak if you do it yourself. Since court filing fees are subject to change and vary from county to county, it is advised you get this information by contacting the *Clerk of Probate Court* in the county where you live. **NOTE:** Many courts will not take a personal check unless it is certified.

**Can I get my name change without a court hearing?**

No—Though the procedure varies between counties, some type of informal hearing will be required and it will be necessary that you attend.

**Will I need any witnesses at the hearing?**

No—However, *you* may have to submit to some short testimony.

**Does an attorney need to sign my forms to make them legal?**

No—It is settled in the law that you may represent yourself.

**Are there any restrictions to my getting a name change?**

Generally, name changes are permitted for "reasonable and proper cause" unless it is being done for a fraudulent or deceptive purpose. These is also a requirement that the person requesting the name change be a *resident* of the county in which the name change is to be brought for a period of *one year* before actual filing.

**May there be other forms that I may need to fill-out for my name change, other than those contained in this LawPak?**

Yes—Once you complete the court phase of the name change, you may wish to have the change accepted by various business and governmental agencies with which you deal. They may require you to fill-out additional forms for their internal use.

Questions 10

**Do I have a problem if I am already using my new name?**

No. The court will usually ask you a question about whether you are already using the name. If you have been using the new name, this is not a problem.

**How long will it take to complete my name change?**

The law first requires that you file your petition for the name change and set a hearing date far enough in the future (approximately four to six weeks) to permit publication in a newspaper of general circulation in the county where the name change is to be filed. Once completed, you must obtain a proof of publication form (the newspaper will either send the form to you or to the court, ask the newspaper about their normal procedure). You will need this proof of publication form before the court hearing.

**Can I get my birth certificate changed?**

Yes. You can send a certified copy of the order changing your name (obtained from the probate court) to the birth certificate registration agency in the state where you were *born*. Usually a nominal fee will also be charged by the court for the certified copy and by the state agency for the change. (Appendix B contains the addresses of the various state agencies).

# A5 Advantages Of Doing Your Own Name Change

### ■ It's Much Cheaper To Do It Yourself

Probably the most obvious advantage to doing your own name change is the savings in lawyer fees. A typical simple name change handled by a lawyer can range in price from $300. to $500. Since the charges for court costs, publication fee and birth certificate change remains constant, the savings can be at least hundreds of dollars.

### ■ The Satisfaction Of Knowing You Did It Yourself

We all receive personal satisfaction in knowing we can accomplish important tasks ourselves. Accomplishing your own name change may be a temporary inconvenience, but you should understand each step in the process, make your own decisions, and control your own life.

#  Required Conditions For Name Change

- In most states, you must have been a *resident* of the county where you live for at least *one year* before filing for the name change.

- You must have a reasonable and proper cause for the name change.

- The name change must not be sought for purposes of deception, fraudulent purpose, or to mislead creditors.

- If a name change is to be sought for a minor child, you will have to prove that the change is in the child's best interest.

- Upon the filing of your name change and obtaining the hearing date, a "Notice of Application" (Sample form contained in the forms section), shall be published *once* in a newspaper of general circulation in the county where you live, at least thirty (30) days before your filing the name change request. The newspaper will give you a "proof of service" that you will need to bring to court with you on the day of the hearing, assuming the newspaper does not send the "proof of service" directly to the court. Be sure that the hearing date is set by the clerk far enough into the future to allow for time to complete the thirty day period needed for the notice in the newspaper.

# Required Waiting Period

In most states the law requires that before there can be a hearing on your request for your name change, there must first be notice of your intent to change your name published in a newspaper of general circulation in your community. After this notice is published you must wait thirty days before you can attend the court hearing to have your name change request heard.

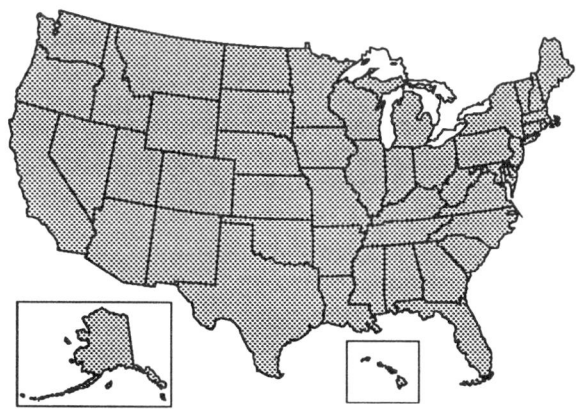

# CHAPTER B

## *Basic Information On Changing Your Name*

 ## Methods Of Changing Your Name

Most of the states have similar laws that govern name changes. Basically, two methods are available. These are the *court proceeding or judicial method* in which one goes to court and obtains an order granting a name change; and the other is known as the *common-law or usage method,* where a person simply adopts a new name or a new spelling of the former name and begins to use the new name. This method is valid as long as the change is done in good faith with no aim to deceive or defraud. However, the common-law method has disadvantages in that it is indefinite (it takes a very long time to accomplish), and it offers no definite way for the person with the new name to "prove" the fact that the change took place. With the many kinds of documents one must deal with in the modern world, this method can cause confusion.

The court proceeding method of name change does not replace the common-law method, but enhances it. It supplies the "proof" of the name change—the court order—which is definite and a matter of public record.

If one uses the common-law/usage method, the key to making the change successful is the consistent use of the new name in all personal, social, and business activities. As a practical matter all government and business agencies must be notified, as well as all friends, and acquaintances. A check list of such government and business agencies is found in the next chapter.

 ## Name Given At Birth

As a matter of custom (practices and culture passed between generations) a person's name usually consists of a given first name, or Christian name and the surname or family name which is passed along from the father to his children. Originally people did not have surnames. This additional name requirement evolved as the need to identify people with more certainty developed. Historically, the middle name or middle initial was not considered part of the official name. However, if the middle name or initial is used, it becomes important as a way to further identify persons, though it may be necessary for a person to prove the middle name as stated.

## B3 Names A Person Cannot Use

The general guideline for name changes is that it not be done for a fraudulent or deceptive purpose. This generally means that if the new name would interfere with the rights of others, or have some other illegal use, it cannot be used. Thus, you cannot change your name to that of some famous person, such as a Hollywood personality or United States President. The goal here is to avoid confusion—or being mistaken for someone else who already uses that particular name you want.

One type of special name which is permitted and which also *is not* a name change involves the use of a professional name. Normally these are commonly found among actors or authors—such as Mark Twain for Samuel L. Clemens or Vickie Lester for Esther Blodgett. It is perfectly legal to use such a stage or pen name—as long as it is not for fraudulent purposes. Additionally, adopting such a name does not have the effect of a name change. Your original name remains your official name. Another example of such a professional name occurs when a woman becomes prominent in her profession before marriage and continues to use her maiden name in her professional life, while using her married or legal name for all other purposes.

If one desires to change his or her name to something unusually creative such as a one word name or description not normally accepted as a name, it is less certain that such a change would receive court approval. There is no clear law on the subject permitting the practice. In such a situation, checking with an attorney before going to court could avoid unnecessary problems.

# B4 Changing Or Not Changing A Woman's Name Upon Marriage

Normally, in the United States, by what amounts to a very strong custom, a woman assumes her husband's surname upon marriage. However, there is no law which requires that this happen. In reality a woman, upon marriage, may either assume her husband's surname or may keep her maiden name. There is no requirement that her name be changed. If it is the wife's desire to continue to use her maiden name, all that is required is that she not begin to use her husband's name and keep the maiden name on all records. It should be kept in mind that the custom which assumes the wife will use the married name is so strong that there are likely to be problems with government and business agencies.

In the situation where a married woman starts the marriage by using her husband's last name, but later decides to change it back to her maiden name, matters are more complicated. Since it is not merely a matter of leaving things as they were, some action by the wife to change the name back is necessary. Due to the confusion that can be caused by this particular kind of change, using the court procedure may be simpler. It does not appear that the husband's legal consent to such a change is necessary, although it should certainly be discussed so as to reduce misunderstanding.

Another possible variation of the marriage name situation is the hyphenated surname, such as husband's name-wife's name or wife's name-husband's name. These kinds of surnames are legal and can be achieved through either the usage or court proceeding methods.

# B5 Divorced Women And Name Changes

At the time of her divorce or dissolution of marriage, a woman can have two options relative to the surname she can use in the future. First, either to continue to use her husband's surname or second, to return to the use of her maiden name. When a name change is done as part of a divorce or dissolution, the fact of such a change is included in the decree. No further proceedings are necessary relative to the name change. If proof of the name change is required, the decree of divorce or dissolution serves as the proving document.

If the divorce or dissolution occurred some years ago and no name change was requested in the decree at that time, it is still possible to change the wife's name using the court proceeding method in Probate Court described in Part II. It is also possible to achieve the name change by the common-law usage method.

Marriage 16

## B6 Changing A Child's Name

In most states, there are specific laws permitting a change of name of a minor. In these situations, a child requesting a name change may do so with an adult applying as the child's "next friend", which is normally one or both of the parents, though having the parents apply is not required. A legal guardian or a guardian-ad-litem (which is a special attorney appointed to represent the child's interest in certain court proceedings) may also file an application. In all cases where a minor's name is to be changed, the consent of both parents is *required*. If the mother alleges someone to be the father, he *must* consent. If the child's birth certificate lists and the mother does not know the identity of the father, then the consent of the parent named in the birth certificate is sufficient. If the parents do not consent, then they must receive notice of the name change hearing, sent by certified mail, return receipt requested.

**NOTE:** If you are requesting the name change of your child/children and the other parent *does not* consent to this name change, we suggest that you seek assistance from an attorney because this procedure can be much more complicated.

If a parent has died, it will be necessary to produce a certified copy of that parent's death certificate for the court. Additional notice similar to that discussed in Chapter A-7 is also required. At the Probate Court hearing, it is necessary that the court make a finding that the name change is in the "best interests of the child" or that the proposed change is to the child's benefit. If it is not, the name change may not be granted.

## B7 Children Of Divorced Parents And Name Changes

One type of name change involving children which causes more litigation than other types of name changes deals with the situation where a remarried divorcee seeks to change the surname of her child/children to that of the new husband. In this situation, often the former husband/father objects and a full court hearing can result. The court applies the standard mentioned previously—"the best interest of the child".

Generally, there is no simple solution to these cases. Such a name change is usually not considered to be in the child's best interest, though exceptions exist. If the noncustodial parent has been guilty of certain types of misconduct, a name change may be permitted. It is best to consult an attorney if you find yourself on either side of this particular situation. **Do not attempt to do such a case yourself.**

# CHAPTER C
## *Getting The Name Change Recognized*

### C1 Governmental Agencies To Notify

Whether you have changed your name by the common-law/usage method or the court proceeding/judicial method, the most difficult obstacle is getting the name change accepted. If you have used the court proceeding method, acceptance is normally easier as you can obtain court certified copies of your name change order and submit these to the various governmental and business agencies as proof of the name change. If you have used the common-law method, it is likely that you will encounter more reluctance to recognize the name change—even though it is legal. It is suggested to begin by using one of your certified copies of the name change order to obtain a new social security card in the revised name, and then use that identification as well as the name change order from the court, to obtain recognition from the other agencies from who the recognition is being sought. Generally, the more official identification documentation of the new name, the more easily you should be able to get other agencies to honor the name change. Certified copies can be obtained from the court where you obtained your name change for a nominal charge.

**NOTE:** Ordering at least five (5) copies at the beginning would be wise.

**a** **Birth Certificates.** Each state maintains a central office of vital statistics, or an equivalent entity, usually located in the state capital. Generally, a new birth certificate will not be issued, but an official attachment will be made to the original birth certificate reflecting that a name change was made. A certified copy of the court order changing the name, along with a registration fee, should be sent to the appropriate central office in the state where you were *born* (not where you currently live). A list of addresses for the various state agencies appears in Appendix B. In order to determine the current registration fee, write the agency for this information before sending the actual application.

**b** **Social Security.** Your local social security office should have available the "Request for Change in Social Security Records" form for you to fill out. Also needed will be one piece of 'acceptable identification' containing your former name (such as an item containing your signature), and a certified copy of the court order changing your name. In the case of a married woman seeking to be recognized under her married name, the marriage license is substituted for the court order and that accompanies the identification of the former name. The authority for this procedure is found in Title 20 of the Code of Federal Regulations, sections 422.107(C) and 422.110, which can be found in most libraries.

**c**   **Driver's License/Car Registration.** Take a certified copy of the court order changing your name to the local Bureau of Motor Vehicles Registrar who will have you sign the appropriate forms and forward them to the central BMV office. Also bring your social security card. Although, most state laws have no provision for changing the name on an auto title (thus, your new name will not appear on your car ownership document until you purchase your next car), the annual license plate registration, upon presentation of a certified court copy of the order changing your name, can be changed to reflect the fact of the new name and the name appearing on the title.

**d**   **Voter Registration.** Again, take a certified copy of the court order changing your name to the main Board of Elections office for your county. They should make the appropriate changes in your records.

**e**   **Federal Income Tax.** If application is made for a change in the Social Security card, this information is automatically forwarded to the Internal Revenue Service. The next time you fill-out your income tax return, use the new name.
**State Income Tax.** Send a letter, including a certified copy of the court name change order to:
    Your State's
    Department of Taxation
Be sure to include in the letter your old name and your social security number. When filing your first state return after the name change, attach copies of this correspondence to the return.

**f**   **Deeds to Real Estate.** It is not necessary to change the deed as recorded. At the time the property is transferred (regardless of how long after the name change is accomplished) a notation can be made on the transferring deed as to the former name and current name. If the property is being probated, an affidavit can be filed by the fiduciary reflecting the name change situation.

**g**   **Passports.** Go to the nearest passport agency with a copy of the court order. If you already have a passport, bring this also. Upon filling out the proper application or amendment form, the passport will be issued in your new name.

**h**   **Welfare Payments.** If you are receiving such payment, take a copy of the court order to the local office. The records should be changed and eventually payments will be made in your new name.

**i**   **Postal Service.** Inform the Postal Service to list both your old and new name for your address.

**j** **Selective Service.** Send a letter containing your social security number, your former name, your new name, and a copy of the name change order to both your local board and:

National Headquarters
Selective Service System
Washington, DC 20435

applying to have the review board recognize the name change. Bringing a copy of the certified court ordered name change would probably help.

# C2 Important Private Sector Entities To Notify

**a** **Mortgages.** Obviously, even after the name change, you are liable for your mortgage. Notify your mortgage company of the change. Although the mortgage recorded at the Courthouse will probably not be changed, the company's records can reflect the new name. Remember, there is no change in the legal obligations imposed by the mortgage.

**b** **Credit Cards.** Notify the companies issuing your cards of the change and request new cards. To protect your credit history, be sure the original date of the account is included with the new name as well as the name in which the account was originally issued.

**c** **Bank Accounts.** Change the signature cards on all checking and savings accounts. No documentation should be required. Also, it will be necessary to order new checks with the new name.

**d** **Stocks and Bonds.** On the face of the stock document the name of the bank functioning as transfer agent will be identified. Your local library should have the address for the bank or unit mentioned. Write that bank or unit care of "Stock Transfer Department", and outline the change you wish to make. You will receive a reply from the bank or transfer unit outlining what must be done and containing the forms to be completed. It normally requires submitting a transfer form containing your signature guaranteed by a local bank. Also required will be your social security number. Complete these forms and return to the stock transfer authority.

**e** **Wills and Inheritances.** Although you may be listed in a Will under your former name, it will not affect your ability to inherit. It would be helpful to notify the executor or administrator of the change as that person may need to file an affidavit with the probate court documenting the name change.

**f** **Insurance.** Basically all that is needed is to notify the various companies of the change. If car insurance is involved there should be no change in rates as these are based upon experience factors. If you are the beneficiary under a life insurance policy the company should be notified in advance, if possible. Otherwise, producing a certified copy of the court ordered name change will probably be necessary at the time you apply for payment.

**g** **Telephone Listing.** Initially, it might be helpful to list both the old and new name. Additional listings in the phone book is available at a nominal charge. No documentation should be necessary.

**h** **School Records.** You should have your schools change the name on your records in case potential employers request copies of your grades. It is also possible to petition to have diplomas and degrees issued in your new name.

**i** **Professional Associations.** All that should be necessary is to notify them of the change.

**j** **Creditors.** Inform your creditors of the name change. A change of name *will not* make your debts disappear.

## C3 Other Records To Change

Examine your valuable papers to determine whether there are other persons or entities important to you which need to be notified. Write them a letter informing them of the name change and whether they require further proof. Usually, the "proof" would be either a certified copy of the court order of the name change, or an unofficial photocopy of the court order.

*Part Two*
*How To Do A Name Change*

# 1

# How To Use The Forms

This LawPak contains one original of each of the forms needed to accomplish your own name change, where forms are not otherwise recommended by the local court. In addition you will need to contact the Clerk of Courts within your county to establish whether there may be additional required or recommended local forms. Sometimes, in name change situations, individual counties stock pre-printed blank forms which are to be used. Generally these forms require the same information as will be discussed in this LawPak, but for sake of uniformity the individual county will request that their local forms be used.

In the following pages you will find SAMPLES of completed forms. These forms are only to serve as a guide to assist you in completing your own name change forms. You must check the appropriate boxes *carefully* and complete the correct information on the original forms which are provided. You may want to photocopy the original forms to better protect against mistakes until you are prepared to type the originals.

Keep your papers safe, neat, organized, and all together in one place.

Other general rules which apply to all forms include:

1. Use a typewriter and carefully proofread each form to be sure all information is correct.

2. Use full names on all papers, be consistent—names should appear exactly the same each time, including signatures. Use name in normal order—last names go last.

3. The Court will always keep the original of each form. You will also need a copy for yourself. Several Counties require the original and additional copies. It is suggested that an original and four (4) copies should be sufficient for most situations. Type each form neatly, check for errors, then have the desired number of copies made. Check the yellow pages for copying and duplicating services in your area.

4. At certain places in the forms you will write your signature on a signature line. This has the same effect as an oath or sworn statement.

*Use of Form* 24

# 2

# Local County Forms

In the United States, Name Change forms have not been standardized. As a result different states may require local forms and guidelines. We do not attempt to keep-up with the local forms and changes, since such local items are subject to change at anytime.

We again suggest you telephone your County's Clerk of Probate Court and check to see whether your county prescribes blank forms on which all name change actions are to be typed. Ask whether the Clerk will mail these forms to you or whether you must personally pick them up and if so, where. Also ask when it must be filed and with whom, and whether you need to contact the newspaper to arrange the publication, or whether the court handles everything.

# 3

# How To File Your Forms And Set Your Hearing Date

This is a very simple process. After you have completed the Petition to Change name, Notice By Publication, and Judgment Entry Ordering Name Change of Adult (This is the court order changing your name referred to in the text), sign the Petition and Notice with your *former name*. Then have four copies of the forms made. Take these, the filing fee and the newspaper fee for the publication (no personal checks) to the Clerk of the Probate Court in your county. Upon filing, you will receive a receipt and be given, or directed to the person who will assign your hearing date, and the name of the court officer hearing it. Remember, you will have previously telephoned the clerk to obtain the correct amount of the filing fee and newspaper fee.

The Clerk will stamp each copy of the documents, and return some to you for your records. In some counties the Court may keep all copies of the Judgment Entry/Orders, while other counties will return all copies to you and instruct you to bring them on the day of the hearing. Be sure you find out which way it is done in your county. Check with the Clerk to determine whether they handle the newspaper publication or whether you must arrange it yourself. If the Court handles it, you need only to pay the publication fee and you are finished. If you must do it, ask what newspapers the Court finds acceptable, then go to an office of *one* of these publications. Present to the newspaper a Court stamped copy of the Notice by Publication (or the original if the Court returns it to you). Make sure that the date of the notice's publication will provide for thirty (30) days before the court hearing.

Also, the newspaper will be preparing an "Affidavit in Proof of Publication (see form in samples) which must be in Court by the date of the hearing. Check whether you will need to pick it up and by when, or whether it will be mailed to you or the Court. If it is not presented to the Court the day of the hearing, your name change will not be granted.

# 4

# The Petition For A Name Change Of An Adult

## WHAT IS IT

This is the form that starts the name change process with the court. It contains your old and new names and the reason why you are requesting the name change. When you sign this form, be sure to sign your *old* name.

IN THE COMMON PLEAS COURT
PROBATE DIVISION
_____Your_____ COUNTY, __Your State__

IN THE MATTER OF )
CHANGING THE NAME )
                 )  CASE NO. __Court Assigned__
                 )
OF __Jack Timothy Ripper__ )
                 )  PETITION TO CHANGE
TO __John Timothy Doe__ )
                 )  THE NAME OF AN ADULT
                 )
    Petitioner   )

Petitioner, __Jack Timothy Ripper__, states that petitioner has been a resident of __Your__, County, __Your State__ for more than one (1) year prior to the filing of this Petition; that is from about the __23__ day of __March__, 19 __85__.

Petitioner further states that petitioner desires to change petitioner's name from __Jack Timothy Ripper__ to __John Timothy Doe__ for the reason that __my current name causes me much abuse, suspicion and ridicule. I desire a more ordinary name.__

__John Timothy Doe__ is the designation that the petitioner prefers.

Petitioner further states that notice will be given according to law; and that a copy of said notice, with proof of publication, will be offered to the Court at the time of the hearing.

WHEREFORE, Petitioner requests that Petitioner's name be changed from __Jack Timothy Ripper__ to __John Timothy Doe__.

__Old Name Signature__
Petitioner

__Your Full Address__

# SAMPLE

IN THE COMMON PLEAS COURT
PROBATE DIVISION
_____Your_____ COUNTY, __Your State__

IN THE MATTER OF:                    )
                                     )   CASE NO. __Court Assigned__
                                     )
___Jack Timothy Ripper___            )
                                     )   SETTING PETITION FOR HEARING

    For good cause shown, the Court hereby orders that the Petition for the change of name filed on __22__ day of ____March____, 19 __93__ by _____John Timothy Doe_____ whose name is currently ____Jack Timothy Ripper____ but will be changed to ____John Timothy Doe____, will be heard on the _____ day of _____, 19 _____, at _____ o'clock _____.
**(court assigns Date and Time)**

                                _____Judge's Signature_____
JUDGE
COURT OF COMMON PLEAS
PROBATE DIVISION
_____Your_____, COUNTY, __Your State__

# SAMPLE

# 5

# Notice Of Publication Of Name Change Of An Adult

## WHAT IS IT

This is the document which you prepare from which the newspaper will print the notice of your name change and constructs it as a legal advertisement. Depending on the procedure in your county, the court may send this to the newspaper or you will need to deliver it to the newspaper. Be sure to ask the Clerk of the Probate Court which process is followed in your county.

# Affidavit
# Name Change Of An Adult

## WHAT IS IT

Some counties *may* require this Affidavit stipulating that you are over eighteen years of age and that you request publication of the notice of the name change. Note that you must sign this document before a notary public, and the notary must then sign in the space provided below your name.

# Entry Ordering Publication
# Name Change Of An Adult

## WHAT IS IT

Some counties *may* require a court order requesting publication. Note that this court order is signed by the judge of the Court of Common Pleas. You do not sign this document, though it may be necessary to prepare such a document for the judge to sign.

IN THE COMMON PLEAS COURT
PROBATE DIVISION
__Your__ COUNTY, __Your State__

IN THE MATTER OF )
CHANGING THE NAME )
 ) CASE NO. __Court Assigned__
 )
OF __Jack Timothy Ripper__ )
 ) NOTICE BY PUBLICATION
TO __John Timothy Doe__  OF CHANGE OF NAME OF
 AN ADULT

> Enter the Name of the Publication which the Probate Court utilizes to Print Notice.

TO: __The Cincinnati Court Index__

__Jack Timothy Ripper__ , residing at __1000 Main Street__ __Your City__ , __State, Zip__ , hereby gives notice that ☒ he/☐ she will file ☒ his/☐ her petition in the Probate Court of __Your__ County, __Your State__ requesting an order from the court permitting the change of ☒ his/☐ her name from __Jack Timothy Ripper__ to __John Timothy Doe__ ; that the petition will be heard on the ____ day of _____ , 19 ____ , at ____ o'clock ____ .
*(court assigns Date and Time)*

__Old Name Signature__
Signature of Applicant

**SAMPLE**

IN THE COMMON PLEAS COURT
PROBATE DIVISION
__**Your**__ COUNTY, __**Your State**__

IN THE MATTER OF:  )
                                )   CASE NO. __**Court Assigned**__
                                )
__**Jack Timothy Ripper**__

                                     AFFIDAVIT

STATE OF __**Your**__ :
COUNTY OF __**Your**__ :

    Now comes, __**Jack Timothy Ripper**__, the Petitioner herein, and being duly sworn, states as follows:

1) That he/she is the Petitioner in the proceedings for a name change and is over eighteen years of age;

2) That the Affidavit request that service of notice be made by publication.

                                                                __**Old Name Signature**__
                                                                 Signature of Applicant

Sworn to and signed before me this _____ day of _____, 19 _____ .
                            ***(A Notary must witness Your Signature)***

                                                                Notary Public

# SAMPLE

IN THE COMMON PLEAS COURT
PROBATE DIVISION
_____**Your**_____ COUNTY, \_\_\_**Your State**\_\_\_

IN THE MATTER OF:                    )
                                     )   CASE NO. __**Court Assigned**__
                                     )
_____**Jack Timothy Ripper**_____ )
                                         ENTRY ORDERING PUBLICATION

For good cause shown, the Court hereby orders that the Petition for the change of name filed on __**1**__ day of __**April**__, 19__**93**__ by __**Jack Timothy Ripper**__ whose name is currently __**Jack Timothy Ripper**__ but will be changed to __**John Timothy Doe**__ after the hearing be published in the __**Your Local Court Index**__ as required by law.

_____**Judge's Signature**_____
JUDGE
COURT OF COMMON PLEAS
PROBATE DIVISION
\_\_\_\_**Your**\_\_\_\_, COUNTY, __**Your State**__

# SAMPLE

# 6

# Judgment Entry Ordering The Name Change Of An Adult

## WHAT IS IT

Once the name change is completed, this document is the official court proof of the fact that your name has been changed. This is the document of which certified copies will be made to send to the various governmental and business entities to obtain recognition of the name change. You should keep one certified copy of this document in your personal records at all times as your ultimate proof of the name change.

IN THE COURT OF COMMON PLEAS
PROBATE DIVISION
__Your__ COUNTY, __Your State__

IN THE MATTER OF )
CHANGING THE NAME )
                                                      ) CASE NO. __Court Assigned__
)
OF __Jack Timothy Ripper__ )
) JUDGMENT ENTRY
TO __John Timothy Doe__ ) ORDERING THE NAME
      Petitioner ) CHANGE OF AN ADULT

*(court assigns Date)*

    On this _____ day of _____, 19 ____, this cause came on to be heard on the Petition of __Jack Timothy Ripper__, for an order and decree of this Court changing petitioner's name from __Jack Timothy Ripper__ to __John Timothy Doe__, and the same is heard on the Petition, exhibits and testimony.

    Whereupon the Court being fully advised that the Petitioner has given notice of the filing of the Petition for the change of name by publication in a newspaper of general circulation in this county at least thirty (30) days prior to the time set for hearing as required by law, and the Court being satisfied on examination of the proof herein filed, that publication was in all respects legally made the same as is hereby approved.

    The Court finds and is satisfied by proof in open court that the facts set forth in the Petition are true and that there exists reasonable and proper cause for changing the name of the Petitioner.

    IT IS THEREFORE ORDERED, ADJUDGED AND DECREED that the name of the Petitioner be and hereby is changed from __Jack Timothy Ripper__ to __John Timothy Doe__, as prayed for.

                                                                              __Judge's Signature__
                                                                   JUDGE
                                                                 COURT OF COMMON PLEAS
                                                                PROBATE DIVISION
                                                                __Your__ COUNTY, __Your State__

**SAMPLE**

# Affidavit In Proof Of Publication

## WHAT IS IT

This is the document that the newspaper (which publishes the notice required by law that you intend to change your name) sends to the court as proof that the publication took place. Although it is *not* necessary for you to complete this form, a sample copy of it is supplied so that you have an idea of *approximately* what it looks like, because it will be necessary for you to have it at your name change hearing. In some counties the newspaper will send this form directly to the court, in other counties it is sent directly to you. **If it is not sent directly to the court, then it is your responsibility to present it to the court on the day of your hearing.**

IN THE COURT OF COMMON PLEAS
PROBATE DIVISION
_____Your_____ COUNTY, _____Your State_____

NAME CHANGE  
FROM: __Jack Timothy Ripper_____  
TO: __John Timothy Ripper_____

CASE NO. _____87-NC-0013_____

AFFIDAVIT IN PROOF OF PUBLICATION

State of __Your State__, __Your__ County, ss

Personally appeared before me, a Notary Public and in and for said county, _____Will B. Hear_____ the Publisher of the _____City News_____, who being duly sworn, says that the attached advertisement was published one time in the _____City News_____ on the __7th__ day of __February__, 19 __92__ (being at least thirty days prior to the __15th__ day of __March__, 19 __92__, the date of the hearing on the change of name as mentioned in said notice). Said publication is a newspaper of general circulation in the county aforesaid.

> **Notice of Hearing on Change of Name**
>
> Court of Common Pleas  
> Probate Division  
> **Your** County, **Your State**  
> In Re: **Jack T. Ripper**  
> Case No. **87 NC 0013**  
> To Whom It May Concern:  
> You are hereby notified that an application was filed in the Probate Court, **Your** County, **Your State**, to change the name of **Jack Timothy Ripper** of **Your** County, **Your State** to **John Timothy Doe**.  
> Said cause will come on for hearing before said Court on **March 15, 1992**, at **9:00 A.M.**  
> **Jack Timothy Ripper**  
> Applicant.  
> **Your City, Your State. February 7, 1992**

_____  
Will B. Hear

Sworn to and signed in my presence this __11th__ day of __February__, 19 __92__.

_____  
John Q. Public  
Notary Public, State of Your  
My Commission Expires May 1, 1998

# SAMPLE

# 8

# The Petition For A Name Change Of A Minor

## WHAT IS IT

This is the form that starts the name change process with the court. It contains the old and new names of the minor and the reason the name change is being requested. Both the child (old name) and the legal parent must sign this form.

# Consent To Change The Name Of A Minor

## WHAT IS IT

As previously mentioned, in all cases where a minor's name is to be changed, the consent of both parents is *required*. If one of the parents does not consent, then the opposing parent must receive notice of the name change hearing. One of these forms is to be completed by each parent, since consents of *both* parents are required by law. Both of these consent forms are to be filed with the court at the same time as the petition.

Again, we suggest that if you are requesting the name change of your child and the other parent *does not consent* to the name change, we recommend that you seek assistance from an attorney because this procedure will get more complex.

IN THE COMMON PLEAS COURT
PROBATE DIVISION
_____Your_____ COUNTY, _____Your State_____

IN THE MATTER OF )
CHANGING THE NAME ) CASE NO. __**Court Assigned**__
)
)
OF ____**Junior Thomas Smith**____ )
) PETITION FOR CHANGE
TO ____**David Thomas Smith**____ ) OF NAME OF MINOR
)
PETITIONER )

Petitioner, ____**Junior Thomas Smith**____, by and through petitioner's parent and next friend, ____**Jane Theresa Smith**____, states that petitioner has been a resident of ____**Your**____ County, ____**Your State**____ for more than one (1) year prior to the filing of this Petition; that is from about the __**5th**__ day of ____**May**____, 19 __**76**__.

Petitioner further states that petitioner desires to change petitioner name from _____ ____**Junior Thomas Smith**____ to ____**David Thomas Smith**____ for the reason that __**I have never felt the designation of Junior to be a proper name. I desire**__ __**a Christian name.**__ _____ _____ ____**David Thomas Smith**____ is the designation that the petitioner prefers.

Petitioner further states that notice will be given according to law, and that a copy of said notice, with proof of publication, will be offered to the Court at the time of the hearing.

WHEREFORE, Petitioner requests that Petitioner's name be changed from ____**Junior Thomas Smith**____ to ____**David Thomas Smith**____.

_____
**Signature of Child**
Petitioner

_____
**Signature of Parent**
Parent and next friend

_____
**Your Full Address**
_____

# SAMPLE

# 10

# What Happens If Something Goes Wrong

A Name Change is a routine process which should proceed without major problems most of the time. However, you will have to be an active participant in the process to ultimately receive a name change whether you use the services of an attorney, or you choose to complete and file the paperwork yourself.

**Before The Hearing Begins**

In the court environment, people who serve the public sometimes forget *how* to serve the public. It normally does not do any good to remind them. If a clerk or bailiff (or even a judge) is less than helpful or polite, just keep *calm,* be *nice,* and calmly *but firmly* pursue your goal. You have a right to be there, and a *right to represent yourself* without a lawyer ("in pro per"). If someone is making the process difficult for you, there must be a reason. You must find out this reason and try to correct the problem. Ask what is the problem, and if necessary, ask to speak to another court clerk or to his supervisor. *Don't get upset.* You can always return to the clerk's office or to court another day. Don't be afraid to ask questions, and always be polite.

> *Note:* The clerks who work for the court *are not allowed* by law to give you legal advice or assist you in completing the forms because they are not attorneys. However, the clerks *can* give you information and direction about filing your name change, and how name change matters are handled. They are required as part of their duties as public servants to give you general information about court requirements.

If a clerk refuses to give you *blank copies* of any required forms, or refuses to tell you where the forms can be obtained (other than through an attorney), request to speak with his supervisor. Most of these local forms are created and printed by court personnel who are paid with tax revenues. It is your right as a U.S. citizen to have access to the legal system (these forms are part of that system) and represent yourself without having to go to an attorney to receive a form, if this is your choice. However, you may have to pay a small fee to cover the cost of printing the form.

Only you can assert your own legal right to self-representation (whether you use a LawPak to assist you or not). If you become intimidated by the system then you may as well be giving up a valuable right and freedom. Generally, you will find that *most* court personnel are very helpful and polite.

In those cases where court personnel withhold forms, are not very helpful, or refuse to speak with you without an attorney, then there must be reasons which influence their actions.

However, you must understand that all procedures and the completion of all forms must be done in the same required legal manner as if an attorney had prepared them. The court does not have one set of laws for a self-help case and another set for a lawyer. The legal process will be the same. If you lack the competence to prepare the forms and handle your own case, do not expect the court to be patient with you. You should pay a qualified lawyer to advise you and prepare the case.

> *Note:* The Internal Revenue Service (IRS) does not refuse to give a tax payer the correct tax form or tell an individual that they *have to go* to a Certified Public Accountant (or to anyone else) to receive a tax form in order to pay taxes. The IRS assumes that the tax payer either has the ability to complete the form properly, or can seek professional assistance from an accountant or tax preparer. The point is, the tax payer has that *legal choice* and access to the system.

**After The Hearing Begins**

This is somewhat of a frightening time for something to go wrong, don't hit the panic button. You can always ask for a continuance of the case. Lawyers do it all the time.

Most people become very anxious at the thought of answering questions in a court environment. There is no reason to be afraid of the court process if you answer the judge's questions honestly, and have prepared your name change paperwork accurately.

You have the legal right to represent yourself. Do not be afraid to express your views to the judge as long as you obey the judge's decisions and treat everyone with respect.

If the Judge or Referee is difficult or refuses to grant your name change, this means that he/she feels you have left out something essential. Ask the Judge or Referee politely, to explain and if you might give testimony to clarify the issue. If things go very wrong and you cannot figure out what the problem is, just tell the Judge or Referee "Your Honor, I request that this matter be reset for hearing at another time, so that I may have time to seek advice." During the next recess, see if the clerk or bailiff can help you, or if necessary ask to see the judge or referee in chambers. Also **double check your paperwork**.

Assuming you have figured out the problem, have your case reset for hearing.

If things go very wrong and you cannot figure out the problem, just tell the judge, "Your Honor, I request that this matter be reset for hearing at another time so that I may have time to seek advice." You can always ask for a continuance of the case. Doublecheck your paperwork, and if you still cannot determine the problem, seek professional advice from a lawyer.

# Check List

This is a check list of the steps you will take in changing your name. Do not use it until you have read this LawPak. Then, as you complete each step, check it off and go to the next one.

☐ You have decided that you want to change your name.

☐ You have been a resident of the county where you live for one year.

☐ You can present to the court a sufficient reason for the name change.

☐ The name change is not being done to deceive creditors or avoid legal obligation.

☐ You have called the Clerk of Probate Court to determine the name change filing fee, whether there are any special local forms that must be used, and the procedure and fee your local county court uses regarding the notice of publication.

☐ If you are doing a *child's* name change, you have contacted the other parent and received their consent to accomplish the child's name change.

☐ You have completed all the forms to initiate your name change case and checked them to be sure all information is correct.

☐ You have filed your case.

☐ You have set the hearing date.

☐ You have arranged for the publication of the court required notice of name change in a newspaper of general circulation in your county (to be printed at least thirty days before the hearing).

☐ You have determined whether the newspaper will send the notice of publication directly to the court or to you.

☐ You have attended your hearing.

☐ You have recorded your name change order with the court.

☐ You have notified the Social Security Administration and completed the appropriate procedures.

☐ You have notified the Vital Statistics Office of the state where you were *born* and sent them a certified copy of the name change.

☐ You have notified the government entities which you need to.

☐ You have notified the business and private entities you need to.

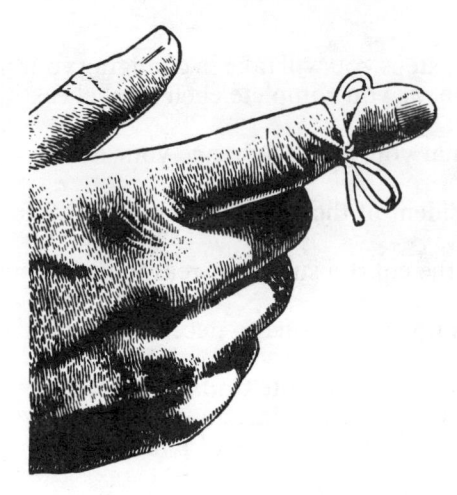

### Special County Requirements

All counties have their own local rules. We have tried to provide you with some basic rules. The **rules can change at any time**, therefore, before filing your petition, we urge you to call the Clerk or take a short trip to the Clerk's office to obtain the proper local forms.

### Definitions

**Paper:** Use our original forms unless your county requires special forms.

**Copies:** Ask the clerk for the number of copies you will need in addition to your original. Remember, you do not file your Entry Order changing your name until the day of the hearing.

**Hearing Date:** Ask the Clerk when filing how to set your hearing date.

# Appendix A

## *How To Get Birth and Death Records*

An official certificate of birth should be on file in the locality where the event occurred. The Federal Government does not maintain files. These records are filed permanently either in a State vital statistics office or in a city, county, or other local office.

To obtain a certified copy of your birth certificate, write or go to the vital statistics office of the State you were born.

To ensure that you receive an accurate record of your birth certificate, please follow the steps outlined below:

- Write to the appropriate office to have your request filled.

- For all certificates send a money order or certified check because the office cannot refund cash lost in transit. All fees are subject to change.

- Type or print all names and addresses in the letter.

- Give the following information:

    1. Full name of person whose record is being requested.

    2. Sex and race.

    3. Parents' names, including maiden name of mother.

    4. Month, day, and year of birth.

    5. Place of birth (city or town, county, and State; and name of hospital if any.)

    6. Purpose for which copy is needed.

    7. Relationship to person whose record is being requested.

# SAMPLE

Date

Your Name
Your Address

Division of Vital Statistics
Ohio Department of Health
G-20 Ohio Departments Building
65 South Front Street
Columbus, Ohio 43215

To Whom It May Concern:

    I am writing to request a birth certificate of one _____**(old name)**_____.
Said child was born on ___**person's birth date**___ to ___**father's name**___ and ___**mother's name**___ in ___**hospital's name**___ at ___**birth city**___ Ohio.

    Enclosed please find a check in the amount of ___**$3.00**___. If there are any additional costs or additional information required, please contact me.

Sincerely,
Type Your Name


Sign Your Name

55    Sample

| Place of Event | Address | Place of Event | Address |
|---|---|---|---|
| **ALABAMA** Birth or Death | Bureau of Vital Statistics State Department of Public Health Montgomery, AL 36130 | **DELAWARE** Birth or Death | Bureau of Vital Statistics Division of Public Health Department of Health and Social Services State Health Building Dover, DE 19901 |
| **ALASKA** Birth or Death | Department of Health and Social Services Bureau of Vital Statistics Pouch H-02G Juneau, AK 99811 | **DISTRICT OF COLUMBIA** Birth or Death | Vital Records Branch 615 Pennsylvania Avenue Washington, D.C. 20004 |
| **AMERICAN SAMOA** Birth or Death | Registrar of Vital Statistics Vital Statistics Section Government of American Samoa Pago Pago, AS 96799 | **FLORIDA** Birth or Death | Department of Health and Rehabilitative Services Office of Vital Statistics P.O. Box 210 Jacksonville, FL 32231 |
| **ARIZONA** Birth or Death | Vital Records Section Arizona Department of Health Services P.O. Box 3887 Phoenix, AZ 85030 | **GEORGIA** Birth or Death | Georgia Department of Human Resources Vital Records Unit Room 217-H 47 Trinity Avenue, SW Atlanta, GA 30334 |
| **ARKANSAS** Birth or Death | Division of Vital Records Arkansas Department of Health 4815 West Markham Street Little Rock, AR 72201 | **GUAM** Birth or Death | Office of Vital Statistics Department of Public Health and Social Services Government of Guam P.O. Box 2816 Agana, GU, M.I. 96910 |
| **CALIFORNIA** Birth or Death | Vital Statistics Branch Department of Health Services 410 N Street Sacramento, CA 95814 | | |
| **CANAL ZONE** Birth or Death | Panama Canal Commission Vital Statistics Clerk APO Miami 34011 | **HAWAII** Birth or Death | Research and Statistics Office State Department of Health P.O. Box 3378 Honolulu, HI 96801 |
| **COLORADO** Birth or Death | Vital Records Section Colorado Department of Health 4210 East 11th Avenue Denver, CO 80220 | **IDAHO** Birth or Death | Bureau of Vital Statistics, Standards, and Local Health Services State Department of Health and Welfare Statehouse Boise, ID 83720 |
| **CONNECTICUT** Birth or Death | Department of Health Services Vital Records Section Division of Health Statistics 79 Elm Street Hartford, CT 06115 | | |

| Place of Event | Address | Place of Event | Address |
|---|---|---|---|
| **ILLINOIS**<br>Birth or Death | Office of Vital Records<br>State Department of Public<br>Health<br>535 West Jefferson Street<br>Springfield, IL 62761 | **MARYLAND**<br>Birth or Death | Division of Vital Records<br>State Department of Health<br>and Mental Hygiene<br>State Office Building<br>P.O. Box 13146<br>201 West Preston Street<br>Baltimore, MD 21203 |
| **INDIANA**<br>Birth or Death | Division of Vital Records<br>State Board of Health<br>1330 West Michigan Street<br>P.O. Box 1964<br>Indianapolis, IN 46206 | **MASSACHUSETTS**<br>Birth or Death | Registry of Vital Records<br>and Statistics<br>150 Tremont Street<br>Room B-3<br>Boston, MA 02111 |
| **IOWA**<br>Birth or Death | Iowa State Department of<br>Health<br>Vital Records Section<br>Lucas State Office Building<br>Des Moines, IA 50319 | **MICHIGAN**<br>Birth or Death | Office of Vital and Health<br>Statistics<br>Michigan Department of<br>Public Health<br>3500 North Logan Street<br>Lansing, MI 48914 |
| **KANSAS**<br>Birth or Death | Bureau of Registration and<br>Health Statistics<br>Kansas State Department of<br>Health and Environment<br>6700 South Topeka Avenue<br>Topeka, KS 66620 | **MINNESOTA**<br>Birth or Death | Minnesota Department of Health<br>Section of Vital Statistics<br>717 Delaware Street SE<br>Minneapolis, MN 55440 |
| **KENTUCKY**<br>Birth or Death | Office of Vital Statistics<br>Department for Human<br>Resources<br>275 East Main Street<br>Frankfort, KY 40621 | **MISSISSIPPI**<br>Birth or Death | Vital Records<br>State Board of Health<br>P.O. Box 1700<br>Jackson, MS 39205 |
| **LOUISIANA**<br>Birth or Death | Division of Vital Records<br>Office of Health Services and<br>Environmental Quality<br>P.O. Box 60630<br>New Orleans, LA 70160 | **MISSOURI**<br>Birth or Death | Division of Health<br>Bureau of Vital Records<br>State Department of Health<br>and Welfare<br>Jefferson City, MO 65101 |
| **MAINE**<br>Birth or Death | Office of Vital Records<br>Human Services Building<br>Station 11<br>State House<br>Augusta, ME 04333 | | |

| Place of Event | Address | Place of Event | Address |
|---|---|---|---|
| **MONTANA**<br>Birth or Death | Bureau of Records and Statistics<br>State Department of Health and Environmental Sciences<br>Helena, MT 59601 | **NEW YORK CITY**<br>Birth or Death | Bureau of Vital Records<br>Department of Health of New York City<br>125 Worth Street<br>New York, NY 10013 |
| **NEBRASKA**<br>Birth or Death | Bureau of Vital Statistics<br>State Department of Health<br>301 Centennial Mall South<br>P.O. Box 95007<br>Lincoln, NE 68509 | **NORTH CAROLINA**<br>Birth or Death | Department of Human Resources<br>Division of Health Services<br>Vital Records Branch<br>P.O. Box 2091<br>Raleigh, NC 27602 |
| **NEVADA**<br>Birth or Death | Division of Health-Vital Statistics<br>Capitol Complex<br>Carson City, NV 89710 | **NORTH DAKOTA**<br>Birth or Death | Division of Vital Records<br>State Department of Health<br>Office of Statistical Services<br>Bismarck, ND 58505 |
| **NEW HAMPSHIRE**<br>Birth or Death | Bureau of Vital Records<br>Health and Welfare Building<br>Hazen Drive<br>Concord, NH 03301 | **OHIO**<br>Birth or Death | Division of Vital Statistics<br>Ohio Department of Health<br>G-20 Ohio Departments Building<br>65 South Front Street<br>Columbus, OH 43215 |
| **NEW JERSEY**<br>Birth or Death | State Department of Health<br>Bureau of Vital Statistics<br>CN 360<br>Trenton, NJ 08625<br><br>Archives and History Bureau<br>State Library Division<br>State Department of Education<br>Trenton, NJ 08625 | **OKLAHOMA**<br>Birth or Death | Vital Records Section<br>State Department of Health<br>Northeast 10th Street & Stonewall<br>P.O. Box 53551<br>Oklahoma City, OK 73152 |
| **NEW MEXICO**<br>Birth or Death | Vital Statistics Bureau<br>New Mexico Health Services Division<br>P.O. Box 968<br>Santa Fe, NM 87503 | **OREGON**<br>Birth or Death | Oregon State Health Division<br>Vital Statistics Section<br>P.O. Box 116<br>Portland, OR 97207 |
| **NEW YORK**<br>Birth or Death | Bureau of Vital Records<br>State Department of Health<br>Empire State Plaza<br>Tower Building<br>Albany, NY 12237 | **PENNSYLVANIA**<br>Birth or Death | Division of Vital Records<br>Pennsylvania Department of Health<br>P.O. Box 1528<br>New Castle, PA 16103 |

| Place of Event | Address | Place of Event | Address |
|---|---|---|---|
| **PUERTO RICO**<br>Birth or Death | Division of Demographic<br>Registry and Vital Statistics<br>Department of Health<br>San Juan, PR 00908 | **VERMONT**<br>Birth or Death | Vermont Department of Health<br>Vital Records Section<br>Box 70<br>115 Colchester Avenue<br>Burlington, VT 05401 |
| **RHODE ISLAND**<br>Birth or Death | Division of Vital Statistics<br>State Department of Health<br>Room 101, Cannon Building<br>75 Davis Street<br>Providence, RI 02908 | **VIRGINIA**<br>Birth or Death | Division of Vital Records<br>and Health Statistics<br>State Department of Health<br>James Madison Building<br>P.O. Box 1000<br>Richmond, VA 23208 |
| **SOUTH CAROLINA**<br>Birth or Death | Office of Vital Records<br>and Public Health Statistics<br>S.C. Department of Health<br>and Environmental Control<br>2600 Bull Street<br>Columbia, SC 29201 | **VIRGIN ISLANDS (U.S.)**<br>Birth or Death<br>St. Croix | Registrar of Vital Statistics<br>Charles Harwood Memorial<br>Hospital<br>St. Croix, VI 00820 |
| **SOUTH DAKOTA**<br>Birth or Death | State Department of Health<br>Health Statistics Program<br>Joe Foss Office Building<br>Pierre, SD 57501 | St. Thomas<br>and<br>St. John | Registrar of Vital Statistics<br>Charlotte Amalie<br>St. Thomas, VI 00802 |
| **TENNESSEE**<br>Birth or Death | Division of Vital Records<br>State Department of Public<br>Health<br>Cordell Hull Building<br>Nashville, TN 37219 | **WASHINGTON**<br>Birth or Death | Vital Records<br>P.O. Box 9709, LB11<br>Olympia, WA 98504 |
| **TEXAS**<br>Birth or Death | Bureau of Vital Statistics<br>Texas Department of Health<br>1100 West 49th Street<br>Austin, TX 78756 | **WEST VIRGINIA**<br>Birth or Death | Division of Vital Statistics<br>State Department of Health<br>State Office Building No. 3<br>Charleston, WV 25305 |
| **TRUST TERRITORY OF THE PACIFIC ISLANDS**<br>Birth or Death | Director of Medical Services<br>Department of Medical<br>Services<br>Saipan, Mariana Islands 96950 | **WISCONSIN**<br>Birth or Death | Bureau of Health Statistics<br>Wisconsin Division of Health<br>P.O. Box 309<br>Madison, WI 53701 |
| **UTAH**<br>Birth or Death | Bureau of Health Statistics<br>Utah Department of Health<br>150 West North Temple<br>P.O. Box 2500<br>Salt Lake City, UT 84110 | **WYOMING**<br>Birth or Death | Vital Records Services<br>Division of Health and<br>Medical Services<br>Hathaway Building<br>Cheyenne, WY 82002 |

# The Blank Forms for Changing the Name of an Adult

1. **Petition To Change The Name of an Adult**
   Gives the court a brief reason why you are requesting the name change.

2. **Setting Petition for Hearing**
   The Court sets the date and time of a hearing at which time the Court will approve or not approve of the name change.

3. **Notice by Publication of Change of Name of an Adult**
   This form gives notice to the local publication that you have filed Petition with the Court to change your name, and you are requesting publication.

4. **Entry Ordering Publication**
   This form is used if your local publication request a Court order to publish the notice of name change.

5. **Affidavit**
   Some Counties may require this affidavit stipulating that you are over eighteen years of age.

6. **Judgement Entry Ordering the Name Change of an Adult**
   Once the hearing has been completed, this is the official proof (signed by the judge), of the fact that your name has been changed.

7. **Required Local Forms**
   Contact your local County Probate Court to obtain these.

*Forms are perforated for easy removal.
Carefully fold and tear along the perforation to remove pages.*

IN THE COMMON PLEAS COURT
PROBATE DIVISION
_____ COUNTY, _____

IN THE MATTER OF              )
CHANGING THE NAME             )       CASE NO. _____
                              )
                              )
OF _____    )       PETITION TO CHANGE
                              )
TO _____    )       THE NAME OF AN ADULT
                              )
    Petitioner                )

    Petitioner, _____ , states that petitioner has been a resident of _____ , County, _____ for more than one (1) year prior to the filing of this Petition; that is from about the _____ day of _____ , 19 _____ .

    Petitioner further states that petitioner desires to change petitioner's name from _____ _____ to _____ for the reason that _____ _____ _____ _____ .
_____ is the designation that the petitioner prefers.

    Petitioner further states that notice will be given according to law; and that a copy of said notice, with proof of publication, will be offered to the Court at the time of the hearing.

    WHEREFORE, Petitioner requests that Petitioner's name be changed from
_____ to _____ .

_____
Petitioner

_____

_____

IN THE COMMON PLEAS COURT
PROBATE DIVISION
_____ COUNTY, _____

IN THE MATTER OF: _____ )
)  CASE NO. _____
)
_____ )
)  SETTING PETITION FOR HEARING

    For good cause shown, the Court hereby orders that the Petition for the change of name filed on _____ day of _____, 19 _____ by _____ whose name is currently _____ but will be changed to _____ will be heard on the _____ day of _____, 19 _____, at _____ o'clock _____.

_____
JUDGE
COURT OF COMMON PLEAS
PROBATE DIVISION
_____, COUNTY, _____

IN THE COMMON PLEAS COURT
PROBATE DIVISION
_____ COUNTY, _____

IN THE MATTER OF )
CHANGING THE NAME ) CASE NO. _____
)
) NOTICE BY PUBLICATION
OF _____ ) OF CHANGE OF NAME OF
)
TO _____ AN ADULT


TO: _____

_____ , residing at _____
_____ , _____ , hereby gives notice that ☐ he/☐ she will file ☐ his/☐ her petition in the Probate Court of _____ County, _____ requesting an order from the court permitting the change of ☐ his/☐ her name from _____
_____ to _____ ; that the petition will be heard on the _____ day of _____ , 19 \_\_\_\_\_ , at _____ o'clock _____ .


_____
Signature of Applicant

IN THE COMMON PLEAS COURT
PROBATE DIVISION
_____ COUNTY, _____

IN THE MATTER OF: )
) CASE NO. _____
)
_____ )
ENTRY ORDERING PUBLICATION

For good cause shown, the Court hereby orders that the Petition for the change of name filed on _____ day of _____ , 19 _____ by _____ whose name is currently _____ but will be changed to _____ after the hearing be published in the _____ as required by law.

_____
JUDGE
COURT OF COMMON PLEAS
PROBATE DIVISION
_____ , COUNTY, _____

IN THE COMMON PLEAS COURT
PROBATE DIVISION
_____ COUNTY, _____

IN THE MATTER OF:                    )
                                     )    CASE NO. _____
                                     )
_____      )
                                          AFFIDAVIT

STATE OF _____     :
COUNTY OF _____    :

    Now comes, _____, the Petitioner herein, and being duly sworn, states as follows:

1) That he/she is the Petitioner in the proceedings for a name change and is over eighteen years of age;

2) That the Affidavit request that service of notice be made by publication.

_____
Signature of Applicant

Sworn to and signed before me this _____ day of _____, 19 _____ .

_____
Notary Public

IN THE COURT OF COMMON PLEAS
PROBATE DIVISION
_____ COUNTY, _____

IN THE MATTER OF )
CHANGING THE NAME ) CASE NO. _____
)
)
OF _____ ) JUDGMENT ENTRY
) ORDERING THE NAME
TO _____ ) CHANGE OF AN ADULT
     Petitioner )

    On this _____ day of _____ , 19 _____ , this cause came on to be heard on the Petition of _____ , for an order and decree of this Court changing petitioner's name from _____ to _____ , and the same is heard on the Petition, exhibits and testimony.

    Whereupon the Court being fully advised that the Petitioner has given notice of the filing of the Petition for the change of name by publication in a newspaper of general circulation in this county at least thirty (30) days prior to the time set for hearing as required by law, and the Court being satisfied on examination of the proof herein filed, that publication was in all respects legally made the same as is hereby approved.

    The Court finds and is satisfied by proof in open court that the facts set forth in the Petition are true and that there exists reasonable and proper cause for changing the name of the Petitioner.

    IT IS THEREFORE ORDERED, ADJUDGED AND DECREED that the name of the Petitioner be and hereby is changed from _____ to _____ , as prayed for.

                                            _____
                                            JUDGE
                                            COURT OF COMMON PLEAS
                                            PROBATE DIVISION
                                        _____ COUNTY, _____

# The Blank Forms for Changing the Name of a Minor

1. **Petition To Change The Name of a Minor**
   Gives the court a brief reason why you are requesting the name change.

2. **Setting Petition for Hearing**
   The Court sets the date and time of a hearing at which time the Court will approve or not approve of the name change.

3. **Answer and Consent to Name Change of a Minor**
   The Court request the written consent of both natural parents in cases where a minor's name is to be changed.

4. **Notice by Publication of Change of Name of an Adult**
   This form gives notice to the local publication that a minor has a Petition filed with the Court to change their name and they are requesting publication.

5. **Entry Ordering Publication**
   This form is used if your local publication request a Court order to publish the notice of name change.

6. **Notice**
   This notice of the hearing is sent to the natural parent of the minor who *has not* submitted written consent of the name change to the Court.

7. **Judgement Entry Ordering the Name Change of a Minor**
   This document is the official Court proof of the fact that the minor child's name has been changed.

8. **Required Local Forms**
   Contact your local County Probate Court to obtain these.

*Forms are perforated for easy removal.*
*Carefully fold and tear along the perforation to remove pages.*

IN THE COMMON PLEAS COURT
PROBATE DIVISION
_____ COUNTY, _____

IN THE MATTER OF )
CHANGING THE NAME ) CASE NO. _____
)
)
OF _____ ) PETITION FOR CHANGE
)
TO _____ ) OF NAME OF MINOR
)
PETITIONER )

Petitioner, _____ , by and through petitioner's parent and next friend, _____ , states that petitioner has been a resident of _____ County, _____ for more than one (1) year prior to the filing of this Petition; that is from about the _____ day of _____ , 19 _____ .

Petitioner further states that petitioner desires to change petitioner name from _____ _____ to _____ for the reason that _____ .
_____ is the designation that the petitioner prefers.

Petitioner further states that notice will be given according to law, and that a copy of said notice, with proof of publication, will be offered to the Court at the time of the hearing.

WHEREFORE, Petitioner requests that Petitioner's name be changed from
_____ to _____ .

_____
Petitioner

_____
Parent and next friend

_____

_____

IN THE COMMON PLEAS COURT
PROBATE DIVISION
_____ COUNTY, _____

IN THE MATTER OF: )
)  CASE NO. _____
)
_____ )
)  SETTING PETITION FOR HEARING

For good cause shown, the Court hereby orders that the Petition for the change of name filed on _____ day of _____, 19 _____ by _____ whose name is currently _____ but will be changed to _____ will be heard on the _____ day of _____, 19 _____, at _____ o'clock _____.

_____
JUDGE
COURT OF COMMON PLEAS
PROBATE DIVISION
_____, COUNTY, _____

IN THE COMMON PLEAS COURT
PROBATE DIVISION
_____ COUNTY, _____

IN THE MATTER OF THE NAME CHANGE OF  :
                                      :  CASE NO. _____
_____  :
                                      :  ANSWER AND CONSENT
                                      :  TO NAME CHANGE
                                      :

    Now comes _____ and represents that I am qualified to consent to the name change of _____ , the petitioner, by virtue of being the natural _____ .

    Being so qualified, I hereby consent to the name change of said child as proposed in said petition and in conformity with the laws of the State of _____ relating to name changes.

    I hereby waive notice of the day set for hearing on the name change of _____ _____ and of any continuance of said hearing. I further represent that the child's name, _____ , is being changed from that to _____ .

_____

STATE OF _____ )
                              ) SS:
COUNTY OF _____ )

    I, _____ , being duly sworn, say that the statements contained in the foregoing Answer and Consent are true and I verily believe.

_____
WITNESS

_____
WITNESS

    Sworn to before me and signed in my presence the _____ day of _____ , 19 _____ .

_____
NOTARY PUBLIC

IN THE COMMON PLEAS COURT
PROBATE DIVISION
_____ COUNTY, _____

IN THE MATTER OF THE NAME CHANGE OF :
: CASE NO. _____
_____ :
: ANSWER AND CONSENT
: TO NAME CHANGE

    Now comes _____ and represents that I am qualified to consent to the name change of _____ , the petitioner, by virtue of being the natural _____ .

    Being so qualified, I hereby consent to the name change of said child as proposed in said petition and in conformity with the laws of the State of _____ relating to name changes.

    I hereby waive notice of the day set for hearing on the name change of _____ _____ and of any continuance of said hearing. I further represent that the child's name, _____ , is being changed from that to _____ .

_____

STATE OF _____ )
                                 SS:
COUNTY OF _____ )

    I, _____ , being duly sworn, say that the statements contained in the foregoing Answer and Consent are true and I verily believe.

_____
WITNESS

_____
WITNESS

    Sworn to before me and signed in my presence the _____ day of _____ , 19 _____ .

_____
NOTARY PUBLIC

IN THE COMMON PLEAS COURT
PROBATE DIVISION
_____ COUNTY, _____

IN THE MATTER OF )
CHANGING THE NAME )  CASE NO. _____
)
)  NOTICE BY PUBLICATION
OF _____ )  OF CHANGE OF NAME OF
)  A MINOR
TO _____

TO: _____

_____ , residing at _____
_____ , _____ , hereby gives notice that ☐ he/ ☐ she will file ☐ his/ ☐ her petition in the Probate Court of _____ County, _____ requesting an order from the court permitting the change of ☐ his/ ☐ her name from _____
_____ to _____ ; that the petition will be heard on the _____ day of _____ , 19 _____ , at _____ o'clock _____ .


_____
Signature of Applicant


_____
Signature of Parent

IN THE COMMON PLEAS COURT
PROBATE DIVISION
_____ COUNTY, _____

IN THE MATTER OF:            )
                                                                            )     CASE NO. _____
                                                                            )
_____ )
                                                                        <u>ENTRY ORDERING PUBLICATION</u>

      For good cause shown, the Court hereby orders that the Petition for the change of name filed on _____ day of _____ , 19 _____ by _____ whose name is currently _____ but will be changed to _____ after the hearing be published in the _____ as required by law.

                                             _____
                                             JUDGE
                                             COURT OF COMMON PLEAS
                                             PROBATE DIVISION
                                             _____ , COUNTY, _____

IN THE COMMON PLEAS COURT
PROBATE DIVISION
_____ COUNTY, _____

IN THE MATTER OF
CHANGING THE NAME

OF _____

TO _____

CASE NO. _____

NOTICE

    Notice is hereby given that _____ , a minor, of _____ County, _____ , through _____ , _____ and next friend will file _____ petition in the Court of Common Pleas, Probate Division of said County, praying for an order of said Court, authorizing the change of _____ name from _____ to _____ ; said petition will be for hearing before said Court on _____ , 19 _____ at _____ o'clock.

_____
a minor, through

_____
mother/father and next friend

IN THE COURT OF COMMON PLEAS
PROBATE DIVISION
_____ COUNTY, _____

IN THE MATTER OF )
CHANGING THE NAME ) CASE NO. _____
)
)
OF _____ ) JUDGMENT ENTRY
) ORDERING THE NAME
TO _____ CHANGE OF A MINOR
Petitioner

On this _____ day of _____, 19____, this cause came on to be heard on the Petition of _____, by and through petitioner's parent and next friend, _____, for an order and decree of this Court changing petitioner's name from _____ to _____ _____, and the same is heard on the Petition, exhibits and testimony.

Whereupon the Court being fully advised that the Petitioner has given notice of the filing of the Petition for the change of name by publication in a newspaper of general circulation in the county at least thirty (30) days prior to the time set for hearing as required by law, and the Court being satisfied on examination of the proof herein filed, that publication was in all respects legally made the same as is hereby approved.

The Court finds and is satisfied by proof in open court that the facts set forth in the Petition are true and that there exists reasonable and proper cause for changing the name of the Petitioner.

IT IS THEREFORE ORDERED, ADJUDGED AND DECREED that the name of the Petitioner be and hereby is changed from _____ to _____, as prayed for.

_____
JUDGE
Court of Common Pleas
Probate Division
_____ County, _____

### Thank You For Purchasing LawPak

We would like to hear from you.

Our goal is to design and develop the best in self-help legal materials. We would like to request your assistance in helping us to accomplish this goal.

Please remove this page from the booklet, complete the below listed information and mail to LawPak, Incorporated. We will then be able to inform you of changes in the law within the next ninety days as these changes may effect the LawPak you purchased. This service is part of our continued commitment to you, the customer.

Also, if you have encountered any new or additional information, forms, problems or processing procedures (not included in this edition) that you think would be helpful to others and should be incorporated into future revised LawPak editions, please take a few moments to send us the form and/or explain the procedure. We welcome your comments and suggestions.

However, we must request that you do not write or telephone LawPak for specific legal advice. As previously discussed, LawPak is organized as a publishing company and cannot by law offer specific advice to individual consumers. If you have specific questions or concerns, please contact a lawyer to advise you.

Name _____

Address _____

City _____ State _____ Zip _____

County _____ Date of Purchase _____ Occupation _____

Title of LawPak _____

Retail Place of Purchase _____

How Were You Made Aware of LawPak _____

Did you find the information in this book helpful? _____

Was it helpful and easy to use this book to accomplish your goals? *(circle one of each)*

*(very helpful)*   1   2   3   4   5   6   *(not at all)*

*(very easy)*   1   2   3   4   5   6   *(very difficult)*

Comments and Suggestions _____

_____

# LawPak®
Inc.

▲ *publishers*

P.O. Box 458
Milford, OH 45150

## Other Available LawPak Self-Help Legal Guides

*Each LawPak contains the court forms, instructions and information to DO-IT-YOURSELF at a fraction of the cost of a lawyer.*

### Valid Throughout The U.S.

- **Last Will & Testament**
One of life's most neglected necessities. Covers provisions for determining beneficiaries, specific bequests, appointing guardians for children and executors for the estate. Appropriate for any marital status and for individuals with or without children.
90 pages ................................................................... $13.95

- **Power of Attorney**
Legally appoint another individual to act on your behalf. Authority may be broad (management of all financial affairs), or limited (sale of house). Also contains Durable Power of Attorney which appoints others to act on person's behalf before becoming incapacitated, thus avoiding guardianship/conservatorship court proceeding.
120 pages ................................................................. $14.95

- **Childrens Emergency Medical Authorization**
Allows parents or legal guardian to legally appoint and authorize adults (baby sitters, relatives, friends, schools, clubs, etc.), to sign for emergency medical treatment for their children when they are unavailable while at work, travel, etc. Includes helpful information for child safety.
72 pages ..................................................................... $7.95

- **Living Will & Durable Power of Attorney for Health Care**
Legally express in writing your preference before maintaining life indefinitely utilizing medical technology and machines when becoming terminally ill or critically injured. Also appoint another individual to make health care decisions for you if you become incapacitated with a Durable Power of Attorney for Health Care.
198 pages ................................................................. $18.95

- **Bankruptcy* Chapter 7**
Will assist a person deciding if Bankruptcy may be a solution to financial problems. Covers debts, property, and legal procedures etc. for filing forms with the bankruptcy court to obtain a legal Chapter 7 Personal Bankruptcy (not for businesses). Appropriate for married couples or individuals.
288 pages ................................................................. $27.95

- **Landlord/Tenant - Rights & Obligations**
Topics covered include the legal rights and obligations of both Landlord and Tenant of residential property (security deposits, liability for repairs or injury, evictions, lease agreements, etc.). Includes a six page written lease agreement, tenant application, and eviction notices.
120 pages ................................................................. $15.95

- **Name Change**
Legally change Adult's or Minor's names due to divorce, remarriage, adoption, birth certificate errors, or personal preference. Allows user to select name which is more appropriate to individuals preference.
92 pages ................................................................... $15.95

### Valid in Ohio

- **Ohio Dissolution of Marriage**
Avoid the expense and time of using an attorney for a NO-FAULT Divorce. Thousands already have! Covers property, debts, custody, support, legal procedures, etc. for filing forms with the court to obtain a legal Dissolution. Appropriate for couples with or without children.
194 pages ................................................................. $24.95

### Valid in Kentucky

- **Kentucky Non-Contested Divorce**
Avoid the expense and time of using an attorney for a NON-CONTESTED Divorce. Thousands already have! Covers property, debts, custody, support, legal procedures, etc. for filing forms with the court to obtain a Legal Non-Contested Divorce. Appropriate for couples with or without children.
180 pages ................................................................. $24.95

---

### Order Form

| Title | Price |
|---|---|
|  |  |
|  |  |

(delivery is by UPS; no P.O. Boxes please.)

**SHIP TO:**

Name_____

Address_____

City_____ State_____ Zip_____

Telephone Number (____) _____-_____

Make *check* or *money order* payable to: **LawPak, Inc.**

Sub Total_____

Ohio Sales Tax (5 1/2%)_____

Postage & Handling____3.35____

**Total Enclosed**_____

*Mail to:*
**LawPak**
P.O. Box 458
Milford, OH 45150

# BILL OF RIGHTS

## *What the amendments say:*

I Congress shall make no law respecting an establishment of religion, or prohibiting the free exercise thereof; or abridging the freedom of speech, or of the press; or the right of the people peaceably to assemble, and to petition the Government for a redress of grievances.

II A well regulated Militia, being necessary to the security of a free State, the right of the people to keep and bear Arms, shall not be infringed.

III No Soldier shall, in time of peace be quartered in any house, without the consent of the Owner, nor in time of war, but in a manner to be prescribed by law.

IV The right of the people to be secure in their persons, houses, papers, and effects, against unreasonable searched and seizures, shall not be violated, and no Warrants shall issue, but upon probable cause, supported by Oath or affirmation, and particularly describing the place to be searched, and the persons or things to be seized.

V No person shall be held to answer for a capital, or otherwise infamous crime, unless on a presentment or indictment of a Grand Jury, except in cases arising in the land or naval forces, or in the Militia, when in actual service in time of War or public danger; nor shall any person be subject for the same offence to be twice put in jeopardy of life or limb; nor shall be compelled in any criminal case to be a witness against himself, nor be deprived of life, liberty, or property. without due process of law, nor shall private property be taken for public use, without just compensation.

VI In all criminal prosecutions, the accused shall enjoy the right to a speedy and public trial, by an impartial jury of the State and district wherein the crime shall have been committed, which district shall have been previously ascertained by law, and to be informed of the nature and cause of the accusation; to be confronted with the witnesses against him; to have compulsory process for obtaining Witnesses in his favor, and to have the Assistance of Counsel for his defence.

VII In Suits at common law, where the value in controversy shall exceed twenty dollars, the right of trial by jury shall be preserved, and no fact tried by a jury, shall be otherwise re-examined in any Court of the United States, than according to the rules of the common law.

VIII Excessive bail shall not be required, nor excessive fines imposed, nor cruel and unusual punishments inflicted.

IX The enumeration in the Constitution, of certain rights, shall not be construed to deny or disparage others retained by the people.

X The powers not delegated to the United States by the Constutition, nor prohibited by it to the States, are reserved to the States respectively, or to the people.

# WE THE PEOPLE.......

Over two hundred years ago, the founding fathers of our nation recognized that while a form of government was necessary, the People would need protection against the awesome power of an unrestrained government. The first ten Amendments to the Constitution of the United States were adopted to provide this protection. These ten Amendments have become to be known as the "Bill of Rights".

What does the Bill of Rights mean to us today?

- It protects your rights to read this book and our right to produce, publish, and distribute it.

- It protects your right to practice the religion of your choice, or if you choose, no religion at all.

- It protects you from unreasonable searches, seizures, and governmental interference.

- It protect you against cruel and unusual punishments, and against unfair arrests and trials.

- It limits the power of the government to those given to the government by the Constitution.

- It protects you from testifying against yourself.

- It guards your individual liberty, guarantees your enumerated rights, and recognizes the need to protect other fundamental rights, although not specifically stated in the Constitution.

**The First Amendment**

The First Amendment guarantees freedom of speech, freedom of the press, freedom of assembly, freedom of religion, and separation between church and state.

This Amendment guarantees your right to speak up and speak out. Benjamin Franklin realized the importance of the fundamental right to freedom of speech when he said, "Whoever would overthrow the liberty of a nation must begin by subduing the freedom of speech."

Both the freedom of speech and freedom of the press are closely related. Just as you can print and speak your mind in all forms, the government may not interfere with the press or censor the news. The government cannot tell the press what it may or may not print.

The freedom of assembly and the right to petition the government are other First Amendment rights that are essential to your fundamental rights of free expression.

In addition, the Bill of Rights protects your religious freedom by protecting you from being forced to practice any religion; by allowing you to practice the religion of your choice, or practice no religion at all; and by mandating the separation of church and state.

## The Second Amendment

The Second Amendment prohibits the infringing of "the right of the People to keep and bear Arms", in order to permit the existence of a "well regulated Militia", which recognizes as being "necessary to the security of a free State". Today, some people believe that this provision means that an individual has the rights to bear Arms, while others believe it only pertains to those in an official "well regulated Militia," and not to the average citizen.

## The Third Amendment

The Third Amendment guarantees that soldiers will not be housed in your home during peace time without your consent, or in time of war except under a specific law.

## The Fourth Amendment

The Fourth Amendment protects you against unreasonable searches and seizures and guarantees your right to privacy.

This Amendment requires that any search or arrest takes place only when a police officer has probable cause which means police officers may not arrest or search you without a direct link between you and the criminal activity. If there is not an emergency situation, they must first obtain search and arrest warrants. These warrants are only issued by a judge or magistrate after he/she are convinced that there is probable cause for such warrants.

## The Fifth Amendment

The Fifth Amendment prohibits denial of life, liberty, or property without the due process of law. It guarantees that if you are arrested, your arrest and trial will be conducted according to established legal procedures. It also protects you against unreasonable police tactics by guaranteeing that you cannot be forced to testify against yourself. This is your right to silence. The government must create their case against you and you do not have to speak to them or assist them in this process.

In addition, this Amendment protects you from being prosecuted by the same sovereign twice for the same crime. It also requires that under the Miranda Rule, that an arresting officer inform you that you have a right to remain silent, along with a right to an attorney, if he/she plans to question you following an arrest.

This Amendment also protects your property from being taken by the government without just compensation.

## The Sixth Amendment

The Sixth Amendment guarantees that you receive a fair trial. It guarantees a speedy, public trial by jury. Also, you must be informed of the charges being brought against you and you must be confronted with the witnesses against you. It guarantees your right to have a lawyer if you are facing a possible jail sentence, (if you choose to have a lawyer). If you cannot afford to hire a lawyer in a criminal case, this Amendment guarantees your right to court-appointed counsel.

**The Seventh Amendment**

The Seventh Amendment reinforces the power of the jury system by guaranteeing that the facts found by a Federal jury will not be re-examined. Once a jury has decided what occurred in a case (the actual facts of the case), another party may not ask for a re-examination of the facts, unless there is no basis in the law for the jury's finding of the facts. The losing party may appeal a ruling, but only on points of law or legal technicalities.

**The Eighth Amendment**

The Eighth Amendment protect you from cruel and unusual punishment; protects you from having excessive fines imposed on you as punishment; and excessive bail as a guarantee of your appearance at trial.

**The Ninth Amendment**

The Ninth Amendment recognizes that the rights granted by the Constitution, including the Bill of Rights and other Amendments are not the only rights that we have as citizens. The Constitution lists many rights and freedoms, but it is not totally inclusive and it would be impossible to list every right. The Ninth Amendment guarantees that these other rights shall not be denied or lessened because they are not enumerated (stated) in the Constitution.

**The Tenth Amendment**

The Tenth Amendment prohibits the Federal Government from exercising powers not given to it by the Constitution. This Amendment reserves any power not given to the Federal Government, and not prohibited to the States, to the individual States, or to the People.

It is our responsibility as citizens to protect, defend, and understand our rights and freedoms given to us by our forefathers and foremothers who in some cases gave their lives in order for us to live in a country where freedom is truly practiced.